MW00875300

NOTED!

A SIMPLE GUIDE TO WRITING AUDIT-FRIENDLY PROGRESS NOTES WITH EASE

AMANDA FLUDD,LCSW-R

ISBN:9798397997751

DEDICATION

This guide is dedicated to all the hard-working professionals who create magic from little and are still asked to do more. I hope this planner helps create more time for all of us in the mental health field.

A special thanks to my close friends, colleagues, and mastermind women who told me to get this done like five years ago and are always available to pour into me (Tamara Dopwell, Katiuscia Gray, Amira Martin, Dr. Corlette Gray, Danielle Slay, Johanna Peters, Dr. Lisa Newland, my Uconn sisters, and so many more).

Definitely grateful for my family, especially my partner Keith, who has been patient with my entrepreneurial crazy and my children. Your love and support, alongside God's grace, make this one beautiful adventure.

Introduction

Progress notes are one of the most essential pieces of documentation for our work, but writing them is the most tedious and avoided task. Over the years, through my journey from intern to private practice owner, I realized that tedious is a complex equation. It is a mix of demands placed on service providers to do life changing work with little time to complete documentation, coupled with a more significant issue of a vague understanding of how to document client progress.

What we don't know, we avoid.
However, as we already know- if it wasn't documented, it didn't happen.

I've lived the vicious cycle of overdue notes and late nights to catch up on documentation with papers sprawled everywhere, with the added fear of being the only clinician cited for an audit hovering in the atmosphere. No one wants to be "that person" caught up in an audit debacle. Nor do we want to be subjected to denied insurance claims, clawbacks, or citations from funders. There is a great deal of professional pressure to get this right.

You've probably fallen into this cycle at some point, as did the hundreds of providers I've trained in documentation and my own clinicians.

You are not alone.

I want to validate that the issue isn't that you don't want to do your notes. The resistance is present because you haven't been trained to write quality notes that reflect the right requirements to avoid professional punishment.

NOTED!

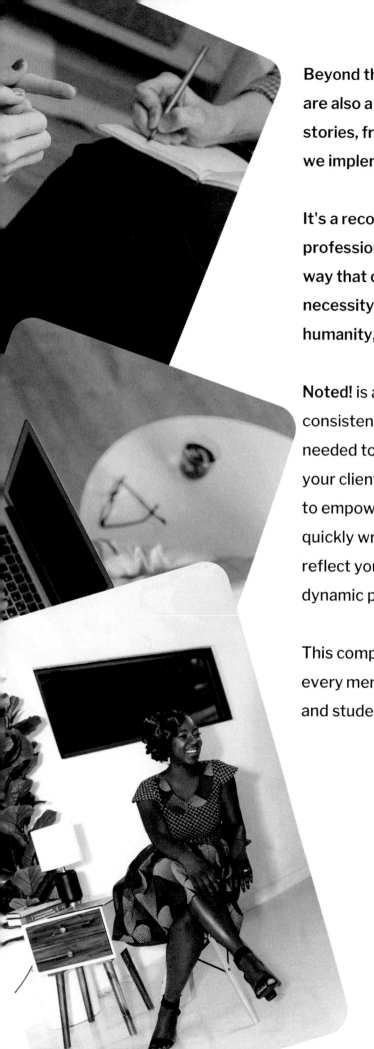

Beyond the technical aspects of notes, progress notes are also a powerful opportunity to document our clients' stories, from their symptomology to the interventions we implement within our scope of practice.

It's a record of their healing journeys and our professional expertise. If we don't tell those stories in a way that creates access to services, demonstrates necessity, or infuses hope with a balance of their humanity, who will?

Noted! is an opportunity to give you a concise, consistent, and accurate format with the language needed to document the progress and challenges of your clients. It's a comprehensive documentation guide to empower your documentation style, allowing you to quickly write clear, concise, audit-friendly notes that reflect your client's journey and your competency as the dynamic professional you are.

This comprehensive guide is a stand-alone resource that every mental health provider, clinical supervisor, intern, and student should have on their bookshelf.

AMANDA FLUDD

FOLLOW ME

@amanda.fludd
@therapyisdope

NOTED!

★ ★ ★ ★ ★

I enjoyed reading the text. It is user-friendly and insightful. The images used throughout allowed the reader to see that the reference guide understands SWs. The format of the texts, style, and fonts was well done. The flow of the information was concise and explained with appropriate examples to assist the reader in understanding the explanations that were provided. This guide is different because it is not overwhelming to go through. It is something to keep close for a quick reference.

Shanique McNeil, MSW

This is very good, organized, understandable, and useful. Thank you for taking the time to pull it together in such a professional way.

Rachel D, Private Practice Owner

Noted! is a practical guide to assist clinicians with the essentials of clinical documentation. Students, new and seasoned professionals will benefit from the guidelines offered. The description of different progress note types and the related examples are an important feature. The narrative writing style of the author is engaging and motivating.

Dr. Lisa Zakiya Newland
Chapter President
Nassau Suffolk Association of Black Social Workers

NOTED!

Table of Contents

Bonus!

NOTED!

A SIMPLE GUIDE TO WRITING AUDIT-FRIENDLY PROGRESS NOTES WITH EASE

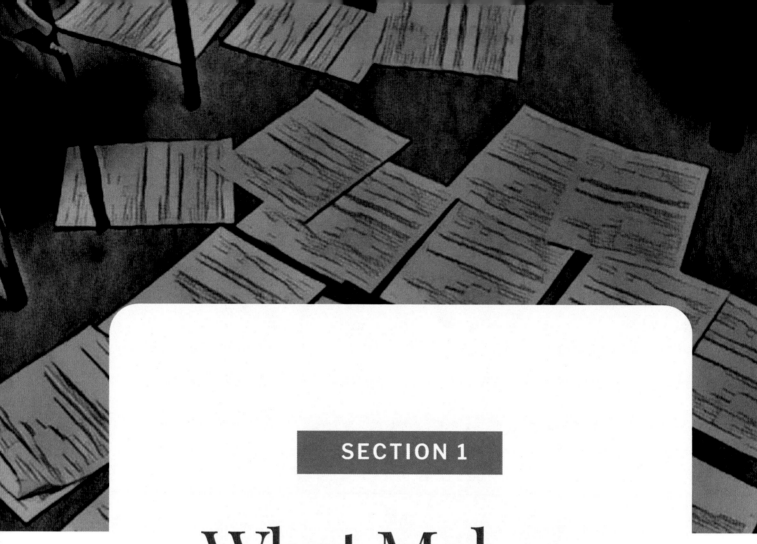

What Makes A Good Progress Note?

What Makes A Good Progress Note?

Section

1

Progress Notes describe the services or interventions provided to the client during the session. It is a legal document included as part of their treatment record. This document allows us to track the individual's progress in treatment and serves as a tool to communicate key aspects of services provided to other providers participating in the individual's care.

Remember that progress notes can be reviewed by your organization and insurance companies, including managed care, auditors, clients, other disciplines, lawyers, judges, or future providers. To effectively communicate with such a diverse audience, it is important that your writing is to the point and easily understandable. Progress notes should embody the language and key principles of quality service provision.

Progress Note
-VS-
Psychotherapy Note

Healthcare professionals usually write progress notes which are part of the client's medical record. These notes are primarily used for communication between healthcare providers, monitoring progress, and legal documentation.

On the other hand, a psychotherapy note is a more detailed and subjective documentation of the therapist's observations, insights, and therapeutic process. Psychotherapy notes are distinct from progress notes and are generally not part of the client's official medical record. They are considered private and personal to the therapist and are often not shared with other healthcare providers unless with the client's explicit consent.

Regarding legal matters, progress notes are more likely to be subject to subpoena. Since progress notes are part of the client's official medical record and contain objective and factual information, they are considered more relevant and admissible in legal proceedings. Psychotherapy notes, being more subjective and personal to the therapist, are generally afforded more protection.

It's important to consult local laws and regulations regarding the specific guidelines for progress notes and psychotherapy notes regarding their potential use in legal matters, as these can vary based on jurisdiction.

NOTED!

The Essentials Checklist:

- THE REASONS FOR MEDICAL NECESSITY IS CLEAR

- DETAILED DESCRIPTION OF SERVICES / INTERVENTIONS PROVIDED

- TREATMENT PLAN GOALS AND OBJECTIVES ARE ADDRESSED

- STATUS AND PROGRESS TOWARDS GOALS ARE CLEARLY INDICATED

- CLEARLY INDICATED START AND STOP TIMES FOR SESSIONS

- INCLUDES ALL PARTICIPANTS OF THE SESSION.

- CLIENT IDENTIFYING DATA IS PRESENT (NAME, DOB, ETC)

NOTED!

"

If it's not documented,
it didn't happen.

-UNKNOWN

NOTES

What to Document

As providers of behavioral health services, we strive to provide quality care to the individuals we serve. Once services have begun, the provider must keep notes on what transpires during each session (as well as pertinent contact notes between sessions). In this section, we will cover the information each progress note should contain alongside the common errors to avoid.

What to Document

Section 2

Most electronic health records (EHR) will include essential client identifiers at the beginning of the note, including the client's name, date of birth, date of session, time, and duration of the session. While the format of the note may vary depending on the EHR used, or the requirements of your place of practice, there are a few sections that are recommended to best organize and structure your note. This includes documenting client functioning, noting their mental status and key symptoms, addressing the purpose of the session, participants involved, the interventions utilized to support change, client response to treatment, and the status of progress toward their goals, as well as the plan for future work, with space for additional comments.

Check List

MENTAL STATUS

Mental status exams are often performed during the first one or two sessions with a client as part of the initial assessment and when reassessing their symptoms. Every note should include a brief description of the client's emotional state.

THEMES & INTERVENTIONS

Indicate the main themes of the session, like trauma, school difficulties, adjustment, etc., and the specific evidenced-based approach provided to support or treat the client.

CLIENT FUCTIONING

A short description of the client's current functioning or subjective concerns specifically impacting wellbeing. What's changed since the last session, severity of issues, list of distress areas or symptoms.

CLIENT RESPONSE & PROGRESS

Describe how the services provided are helping to reduce impairment, improve functioning, or prevent decline. Share what progress looks like and the client's responses to interventions.

PARTICIPANTS

Who the service was provided to (ie, the client) or with (parent, case planner, etc.)

PLAN OF ACTION

What will the client or provider work on between sessions? What is next in treatment or any changes to the treatment plan should also be noted.

Mental Status

These examples represent a range of mental states that may present during therapy or counseling sessions. Providers can use these descriptions to document and monitor changes in the client's mental state, tailor interventions, discuss cases, and track progress over time.

- Improved insight into their thoughts and behaviors.
- Demonstrates concrete thinking with decreased distractibility.
- Exhibiting deficits in reality testing, such as difficulty differentiating between reality and fantasy.
- Displaying features of magical thinking, such as belief in supernatural powers or unrealistic associations.
- Presenting with suicidal ideation or thoughts of self-harm.
- Showing some capacity for reflection and introspection.
- Experiencing racing thoughts or a flight of ideas.
- Expressing feelings of worthlessness or extreme guilt.
- Demonstrating reduced motivation and anhedonia (lack of pleasure or interest).
- Presents with dissociative, hypomanic, manic features, etc.
- Experiencing auditory or visual hallucinations.
- Exhibiting psychomotor agitation or retardation.
- Displaying poor concentration and attention span.
- Demonstrating a heightened sense of anxiety or panic as evidenced by . . .
- Expressing significant changes in appetite or sleep patterns.
- Exhibiting disorganized speech or disorganized behavior.
- Improved judgment.
- Poor capacity for self-reflection.

NOTED!

Client Functioning

These examples represent various ways to describe the client's functioning. This is often found in the subjective section of the note.

- "It's been hard for me to sleep and stop thinking about losing my dad. I'm not sure why I should be here."
- "I'm starting to feel more depressed." The client noted concerns about her mood, endorsing depressed mood, trouble falling asleep, and isolation from friends and family.
- Serious difficulty maintaining self-care and activities of daily living. Moderate impairment in social, work/school functioning.
- Kendal shared that he is " feeling better." He has been sleeping 7-8 hours per night and has been exercising 1-2 times during the week, and is less anxious at work.
- The client reports intrusive thoughts and expressed concern about their inability to stay focused and complete tasks.
- Parent shared child is having trouble listening, completing everyday tasks, and isn't socializing as much with peers. The client shared he feels "alone and sad."
- "I am worried I am taking on more responsibilities and neglecting my own needs." The client discussed challenges in maintaining healthy boundaries and strained relationships with family members and close friends.
- John's depression symptoms significantly affected his ability to carry out routine activities of daily living. He reported experiencing difficulty with self-care tasks, such as maintaining personal hygiene, preparing meals, and completing household chores.

NOTED!

Affect Language

These examples of affective states reflect a range of emotional experiences that clients may express during therapy or counseling sessions that can be included in your notes. It's essential for professionals to assess and monitor these states to understand the client's emotional well-being and guide appropriate interventions.

- Moderately depressed
- Mildly depressed
- Calm and reflective
- Quietly anxious
- Talkative
- Labile (emotional instability)
- Irritable
- Angry
- Excited
- Generally content
- Overwhelmed
- Nervous
- Anxious
- Moderately Anxious
- Hopeful
- Apathetic
- Anhedonic (lack of pleasure or interest)
- Restless
- Agitated
- Despairing (loss of all hope)

- Indifferent
- Energized
- Melancholic
- Withdrawn
- Elated
- Disinterested
- Flat
- Irrational
- Dissociated
- Tired
- Tearful
- Frustrated
- Uneasy
- Resigned
- Distracted
- Inattentive
- Preoccupied
- Numb
- Regressed
- _____
- _____

Session Themes

Identity Themes:

- Self-esteem and self-worth
- Exploration of Gender Identity and family dynamics
- Sexual orientation exploration
- Cultural or racial identity conflicts
- Body image and appearance concerns
- Identity Development in Adolescence
- Identity crises or confusion
- Identity Integration in multicultural contexts
- Identity shifts due to life transitions
- Imposter syndrome
- Navigating guilt around success and achievement

Relational Themes:

- Family conflicts
- Intimacy and relationship issues
- Attachment difficulties
- Interpersonal communication problems
- Setting boundaries
- Trust and betrayal issues
- Codependency patterns
- Social isolation / social anxiety and loneliness
- Co-parenting challenges
- Cultural or intercultural relationship issues
- Guilt and shame around upbringing and dissolving family relationships

Session Themes

Trauma Themes:

- Resolving childhood trauma and abuse
- Difficulty expressing stressful experiences
- Traumatic grief and loss
- Complex trauma and dissociation
- Vicarious trauma or compassion fatigue
- Trauma-related somatic symptoms
- Trauma triggers and flashbacks
- Microaggressions
- Trauma recovery and resilience
- Somatic responses (headaches, jumpiness, GI issues, etc.)
- Trauma-related trust or body related issues
- Navigating end-of-life anxieties and recent loss
- Emotional regulation difficulties post-trauma

Life Stress Themes:

- Work-related stress and burnout
- Financial stress and economic hardships
- Academic or career transitions
- Parenting stress and challenges
- Chronic illness or disability adjustments
- Caregiver stress and role strain
- Relocation or cultural adjustment stress
- Major life changes and transitions
- Loss and grief from significant events
- Balancing multiple life responsibilities

NOTED!

"Challenges make you discover things about yourself that you never really knew."

CICELY TYSON

Intervention Words For Progress Notes

- Actively listened
- Asked
- Assisted client in
- Acknowledged
- Affirmed
- Assessed
- Challenged
- Clarified
- Coached
- Collaborated
- Confronted
- De-escalated
- Demonstrated
- Developed a plan for
- Directed
- Discussed
- Encouraged
- Explained
- Examined
- Explored
- Evaluated
- Facilitated discussion
- Focused on
- Gave homework
- Guided
- Instructed
- Interpreted
- Introduced
- Inquired about
- Led
- Linked
- Listed
- Listened
- Managed
- Measured progress
- Modified
- Mindfulness Based
- Normalized
- Paraphrased
- Performed
- Planned
- Practiced
- Praised
- Prompted
- Provided
- Psychoeducation
- Recommended
- Redirected
- Reflected
- Reframed
- Refocused
- Reinforced
- Revised
- Set boundaries
- Shared
- Summarized
- Supported
- Trained
- Tracked progress
- Validated

NOTED!

COMMON ERRORS CHEAT *Sheet*

Length of Notes

NOTES ARE A NOVEL
NOTES ARE TO VAGUE

Includes Assumptions

PROGRESS NOTES
SHOULD AVOID
PERSONAL JUDGMENTS

Missing Medical Necessity

INCLUDE SYMPTOMS AND
IMPAIRMENTS TO JUSTIFY
SERVICES

Duplicate Note

AVOID COPYING NOTES,
NEGLECTING TO CHANGE
NOTE OR COPYING
DIRECTLY FROM
PLANNERS

Confirmed Late or No Signature

TIME MATTERS FOR
AUDITS AND SIGNATURES
FOR VALIDATION

Time Doesn't Match Billing Code

DOUBLE CHECK
START/ STOP TIMES
AND BILLING CODES

NOTES

How to Organize Your Progress Notes

How to Organize Your Progress Note

Section

3

There are several types of progress note formats that mental health professionals can utilize to write notes efficiently while still ensuring that all necessary key points are included.

Three Common Styles:

- **DAP Note** (Description, Assessment, Plan)
- **SOAP Note** (Subjective, Objective, Assessment, Plan)
- **SIRP Note** (Situation, Intervention, Response, Plan)

What style you use, unless directed by your place of practice, isn't as important as the information captured. I encourage you to find the format that reflects your strengths and comfort levels as a note-taker. If you find these formats restrictive, you can create a customized and more eclectic template that includes all the essential factors without the constraints of fitting them into predefined categories.

NOTED!

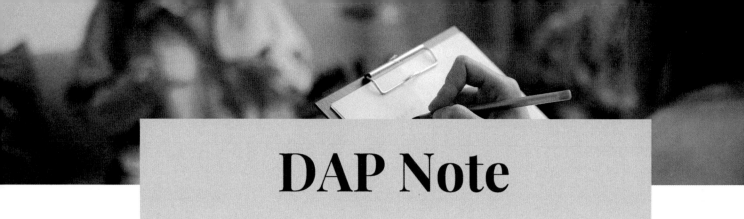

DAP Note

DATA

Observations of the client (appearance, thinking, behavior, mood); information relevant to treatment or that impact diagnosis (symptoms, problems with functioning); and the general focus of the session.

Example: Jada and her mother entered the session and engaged in conversation. The parent was eager to share the client's difficulty listening at home.

ASSESSMENT

This space is for the therapist's professional evaluation and analysis of the client's progress and current mental health status. It may include diagnostic impressions, observations, clinical assessments, and any changes in the client's condition or functioning. Also, a good place to note interventions and the client's response to treatment.

Example: Jada's mother expressed frustration with her behavior, including difficulty listening and focusing. The client administered the PHQ9 returning a score of x, indicating y.

PLAN

The plan section outlines the therapist's or client's action items between sessions. It includes the strategies and techniques that will be implemented to address the client's concerns, as well as any modifications or adjustments to the existing treatment plan.

Example: The client was given homework to practice deep breathing exercises to improve concentration. Follow-up session in two weeks to assess progress and adjust interventions if necessary.

NOTED!

SOAP Note

SUBJECTIVE

This section captures the client's subjective experiences, thoughts, and feelings as reported by the client or observed by the therapist.

Example: The client reported feeling overwhelmed and anxious because of work-related stress. The client mentioned experiencing difficulty sleeping and increased irritability. "I'm starting to feel more depressed."

OBJECTIVE

The objective section includes factual and observable information gathered during the session, assessments, and clinical observations.

Example: The client demonstrated poor eye contact and fidgeting during the session.

ASSESSMENT

Therapist's professional evaluation and analysis of the client's progress and current mental health status. It may include diagnostic impressions, observations, clinical assessments, and changes in the client's condition or functioning. Note interventions and the client's response to treatment.

Example: The client is experiencing symptoms consistent with generalized anxiety disorder. The client's functioning appears to be moderately impacted by anxiety.

PLAN

The Plan section outlines the therapist's or client's action items between sessions. Same as the DAP note.

Example: John will practice deep breathing exercises to improve concentration. Therapist to research social skills groups for clients.

NOTED!

SIRP Note

SUBJECTIVE

The subjective section captures the client's subjective experiences, thoughts, and feelings as reported by the client or observed by the therapist.

Example: Client reported feeling overwhelmed and stressed due to recent work-related demands and relationship conflicts

INTERVENTION

The Intervention section describes the specific therapeutic interventions or techniques (CBT, EMDR, Play Therapy, etc.) used during the session and any administered assessments like the PHQ9.

Example: The Therapist used cognitive-behavioral techniques to help the client challenge negative thoughts and develop coping strategies.

RESPONSE

The client's responses to intervention can be documented here.

Example: The client actively engaged in the session and expressed an understanding of cognitive distortions. Demonstrated improved self-awareness and willingness to practice the coping skills discussed.

PLAN

The plan section outlines the therapist's or client's action items between sessions or any changes to the treatment plan. Same as other note styles.

Example: Couples session scheduled for next week. The therapist encouraged the client to practice relaxation exercises at home at least three times this week and provided resources on stress management.

Let's Practice

Think about a recent client interaction and pick one of the formats to write out your notes on the following practice pages.

Three Common Styles:
- **DAP Note** (Description, Assessment, Plan)
- **SOAP Note** (Subjective, Objective, Assessment, Plan)
- **SIRP Note** (Situation, Intervention, Response, Plan)

⭐ You can reference session themes from pages 20-21.

⭐ Note client functioning from notes on Page 18.

⭐ Improve clinical language with descriptive intervention words from page 23.

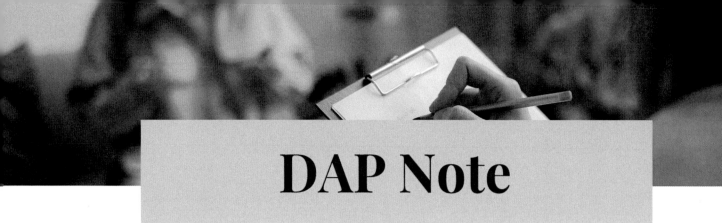

DAP Note

DATA

Observations of the client (appearance, thinking, behavior, mood); information relevant to treatment or that impact diagnosis (symptoms, problems with functioning); and the general focus of the session.

ASSESSMENT

Evaluations, current MSE, diagnostic impressions, observations, clinical assessments, interventions, and the client's response to treatment.

PLAN

Therapist's or client's action items between sessions, any modifications or adjustments to the existing treatment plan, client HW, etc.

NOTED!

SOAP Note

SUBJECTIVE

The client's subjective experiences, thoughts, and feelings as reported by the client.

OBJECTIVE

Observable information, assessments, and clinical observations.

.

ASSESSMENT

Evaluation and analysis of the client's progress, MSE, diagnostic impressions, observations, clinical assessments, and changes in the client's condition or functioning. Interventions and the client's response to treatment.

PLAN

Therapist's or client's action items between sessions, any modifications or adjustments to the existing treatment plan, client HW, etc.

SIRP Note

SUBJECTIVE

The client's subjective experiences, thoughts, and feelings as reported by the client or observed by the therapist.

INTERVENTION

Specific therapeutic interventions or techniques (CBT, EMDR, Play Therapy, etc.) used during the session / administered assessments.

RESPONSE

The client's responses to interventions.

PLAN

Therapist's or client's action items between sessions, any modifications or adjustments to the existing treatment plan, client HW, etc.

NOTES

The Issue of How Much Is Enough

The Issue of How Much Is Enough

Section

4

Writing progress notes is about balancing sufficient information and avoiding unnecessary narrative details. It's important to focus on concise and relevant information, use objective language, and prioritize medical necessity by including diagnosis-related information (like symptoms).

Your goal is to focus on the core points that support measurable goals, medical necessity, and the client's diagnosis.

Avoid excessive narrative or irrelevant details, including judgments, personal bias, or overgeneralizations. Describe the client's behaviors, thoughts, and emotions accurately and precisely.

NOTED!

LET'S PRACTICE:
WHAT NEEDS TO COME OUT?

Check off the boxes for the corresponding sentences that you think don't belong in the note.

- ☐ Jada and her mom arrived for the session and sat separately in the waiting room.
- ☐ As Ms. Louis entered the therapy room, she expressed her frustration with Jada's behavior.
- ☐ "It's as frustrating as trying to find parking by your office. I'm overwhelmed!"
- ☐ This Writer reminded Mom about their psychotherapy homework to engage in uninterrupted active listening exercises outlined last week.
- ☐ Jada rolled her eyes a few times as Mom's cell phone went off, and she quickly answered calls from work.
- ☐ Jada was asked to share her experiences with spending quality time during the week.
- ☐ "Well, I have a lot going on, Ms. Wallace, with my own schedule."
- ☐ "I have track practice, trying to perfect my cake recipes, and catching up on Bridgeton."
- ☐ Writer reflected back on some of the challenges around time and creating space for conversations to improve their relationship and reduce conflict. We used the session to brainstorm challenges and set specific times to work on communicating with each other.
- ☐ Eight minutes into the task, Mom interrupted, saying she had to go to the bathroom.
- ☐ Jada was visibly upset with the disruptions during the session.
- ☐ When her mom returned, we took a moment.
- ☐ The client was helped to express her thoughts and feelings, and the parent was asked to reflect child's concerns using clear communication skills from last week's session.
- ☐ Parent able to engage in eye contact and reflect back accurately and with empathy.
- ☐ The therapist suggested that during the coming week, Mom focus on noticing the times she is distracted and to be intentional with agreed times to practice communication exercises.
- ☐ Mom said she thinks this is something she can do.
- ☐ Jada sipped on her Ice Caramel Latte.
- ☐ Jada then responded that she thinks they can work on this plan.

NOTED!

TRIM THE EXCESS:

Here is what the note could look like below. Keep in mind that depending on your area of practice, some details may need to stay. The idea is to keep the note focused and move away from a long detailed narrative that does not support medical necessity or treatment goals.

- ▨ Jada and her mom arrived for the session and sat separately in the waiting room.

- ▨ As Ms. Louis entered the therapy room, she expressed her frustration with Jada's behavior.

- ✘ "It's as frustrating as trying to find parking by your office. I'm overwhelmed!"

- ▨ This Writer reminded Mom about their psychotherapy homework to engage in uninterrupted active listening exercises outlined last week.

- ✘ Jada rolled her eyes a few times as Mom's cell phone went off, and she quickly answered calls from work.

- ▨ Jada was asked to share her experiences with spending quality time during the week.

- ▨ "Well, I have a lot going on, Ms. Wallace, with my own schedule."

- ✘ "I have track practice, trying to perfect my cake recipes, and catching up on Bridgeton."

- ▨ Writer reflected back on some of the challenges around time and creating space for conversations to improve their relationship and reduce conflict. We used the session to brainstorm challenges and set specific times to work on communicating with each other.

- ✘ Eight minutes into the task, Mom interrupted, saying she had to go to the bathroom.

- ▨ Jada was visibly upset with the disruptions during the session.

- ✘ When her mom returned, we took a moment.

- ▨ The client was helped to express her thoughts and feelings, and the parent was asked to reflect child's concerns using clear communication skills from last week's session.

- ▨ Parent able to engage in eye contact and reflect back accurately and with empathy.

- ▨ The therapist suggested that during the coming week, Mom focus on noticing the times she is distracted and to be intentional with agreed times to practice communication exercises.

- ▨ Mom said she thinks this is something she can do.

- ✘ Jada sipped on her Ice Caramel Latte.

- ▨ Jada then responded that she thinks they can work on this plan.

NOTED!

NOTES

How to Save Time Writing Notes

How to Save Time When Writing Notes

Timely documentation of notes is crucial for several reasons.

First, it ensures accuracy and reliability by capturing the session details while they are still fresh in the provider's memory.

Second, it allows for effective communication and continuity of care among the healthcare professionals involved in the client's treatment.

Third, timely documentation facilitates billing and reimbursement processes, helping providers receive proper compensation for their services.

Fourth, documenting interventions, assessments, and informed consent promotes legal and ethical compliance.

Maintaining time frames for completing notes can be challenging, but it is your ethical and professional responsibility. You can save time on documentation by implementing collaborative notes, where the provider and client document progress in session as part of their wrap-up tasks and reflections. Providers can also save time by utilizing pre-designed templates or electronic health record (EHR) systems for easy access and organization.

NOTED!

timing is everything

Time Managemet

Navigating notes and other responsibilities can be challenging. On the following few pages of Noted!, you'll find productivity charts that you can use to plan out your monthly goals around documentation. Additionally, I've included weekly focus areas that give you space to prioritize notes and important client or work-related tasks.

Experiment with approaches:
- Practice ending sessions 10 mins early to review sessions with clients and write a collaborative note.
- Utilize voice notes to create a written format you can copy and paste.
- Schedule time for notes like you would a session.

Productivity is never an accident. It is always the result of a commitment to excellence, intelligent planning, and focused effort. PAUL J. MEYER

NOTED!

43

Monthly goals

MAIN FOCUS

ACTUAL GOALS

- [ ] _____
- [ ] _____
- [ ] _____

- [ ] _____
- [ ] _____
- [ ] _____

NOTED!

NOTED!

Action Plan
Weekly

DAY 1 | MON

DAY 2 | TUE

DAY 3 | WED

DAY 4 | THU

DAY 5 | FRI

NOTED!

Focus Chart

1	FOCUS 1
2	FOCUS 3
3	FOCUS 5
4	FOCUS 2
5	FOCUS 4
6	FOCUS 6

NOTED!

NOTES

Documenting Risk

Documenting Risk

Section

6

Notes should also be guided by the client's progress toward their treatment plan goals and any changes in their condition that impact the treatment plan.

Any changes regarding risk (suicide, running away, potential harm to self or others, medication events, etc.) should be documented immediately.

When documenting client risk, use clear, concise language that accurately describes the severity of the issue. Where appropriate, document the client's safety plan, outlining specific steps discussed and agreed upon to address and manage the risk. This may involve identifying support networks, crisis hotlines, coping strategies, and emergency contacts.

NOTED!

The longer you wait to document an issue, the more likely it becomes a professional risk and a lost opportunity to resolve it safely.

AMANDA FLUDD, LCSW-R

NOTED!

NOTES

Frequently Asked Questions

Frequently Asked Questions

Section 7

When it comes to documenting progress notes, these are a few of the questions I've received over the years while training providers and organizations. **If your question isn't here,** feel free to email me at: support@amandafludd.com.

1. How often should we document progress notes?

The frequency of documentation can vary depending on factors such as the client's treatment plan, the intensity of therapy, critical changes in client care, and regulatory or organizational requirements. Therapists are generally advised to document progress notes after each session or at regular intervals to ensure accurate and up-to-date information.

2. I tried a collaborative note with a client, and they were offended because I was taking notes in the session. I felt bad after that and stopped. How should I handle a situation like this?

Our clients don't understand the scope of our responsibilities and why the approach may be helpful. You can explain to them how important it is for you to remember the work you are doing with them or for you both to reflect on what happened in the session to ensure you are both on the same page. If you explain the value to the client, they should be invested in this part of the healing process as well.

3. What if the client really isn't making progress, and it's hard to change the note?

Notes can be used to document that the client isn't making progress. It may be a good time to explore why and what is needed to address that, which should be documented. Using progress note planners may be helpful here to expose yourself to wider clinical language to support your writing or descriptive style.

4. Do we need more than one intervention in a note?

It isn't about counting the number of interventions but the quality and the client's responsiveness to them. If that is documented well, you won't have a problem in this area. Some aspects of the work can take longer. For example, if the client had a difficult week and is overwhelmed in session,

NOTED!

maybe all you can do is focus on relaxation strategies to help them regulate their emotions.At the same time, even within that, there may be other interventions utilized, such as active listening, modeling several coping strategies, reviewing triggers and responses, and so on. So naturally, even if the session feels limited because of that one issue that entered the space, you can still document several interventions. I've never participated in a CMS or similar audit and watched the reviewer count the number of interventions used. I recommend focusing more on documenting the quality of work instead of being stuck on the number of things that need to happen in a session.

5. Can progress notes be subpoenaed in a legal proceeding?

Progress notes can be subpoenaed in a legal proceeding. However, I would like to point out that the release of client records is subject to legal and ethical guidelines, including client confidentiality and privacy laws. Sometimes they will allow a clinical summary instead of all of the notes. It's helpful to consult with your organization's legal team or the lawyer associated with your malpractice insurance or professional association for support.

6. Do we have to keep progress notes for a certain amount of time?

Yes. Each state usually has requirements on the time frame to keep progress notes. This allows for the availability of client records for treatment purposes, continuity of care, and potential legal or ethical considerations. It is essential to consult local regulations, professional guidelines, and organizational policies to determine the specific retention period for progress notes in your practice setting.

7. Should we use ChatGPT to write progress notes?

The decision to use ChatGPT or any AI system to write progress notes should be made carefully considering its limitations in accuracy, client confidentiality (it's not a HIPPA-compliant platform), and potential ethical implications. Therapists are responsible for ensuring the accuracy, relevance, and appropriateness of progress notes. It may be a good resource for organizing ideas and quickly completing notes. However, AI-generated notes without therapist input may undermine the therapeutic process and documentation quality.

Bonuses & Templates

CHAT GTP Guide

Bonus

Now that you have a base understanding of progress notes and what should be included, you can use that to work with Ai platforms to document notes quickly and assess for effectiveness.

For a list of prompts to assist the platform in formatting and creating notes closer to guidelines, scan the QR code below for a printable resource.

Keep in mind that the decision to use ChatGPT or any AI system should be based on a thoughtful assessment of the benefits, risks, and ethical considerations in the specific context of the therapy practice. It may be helpful to consult with colleagues, professional organizations, and legal advisors to inform your decision.

Some practices to keep in mind:
- Do not include client-identifying data like name.
- Remember that it is not a confidential platform, and details can be shared for research purposes.
- You should fact-check what is created regarding treatment interventions and processes in the note or suggestions for interventions and treatment.
- Stay informed on updates and changes so you can continue to make ethical decisions in this area.
- Even with the advancement of technology, your brilliance and expertise matter. Don't give that power away.

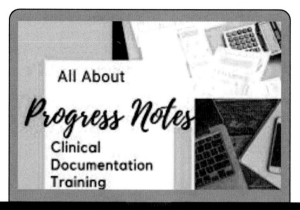

NEED MORE?

Take your progress note skills to the next level with our exclusive on-demand training:

All About Progress Notes

This on-demand training will give you valuable insights into best practices for writing progress notes. Learn how to capture essential information and understand the key elements that support measurable goals and medical necessity. It gives more depth to the concepts in Noted! and takes your confidence to the next level as a provider.

Additional training for organizations, practices, or teams:

- **Clinical Documentation (Progress Notes & Treatment Plans)**
- **Overview of Anxiety**
- **Mental Health 101**
- **Trauma Informed Care**

CONTACT: SUPPORT@AMANDAFLUDD.COM
WWW.AMANDAFLUDD.COM

Client: Time: to:

Session Date: Code:

                                 Next Session:

Session Focus

1

2

Client Data *(Symptoms, MSE, Impact*   Interventions / Concerns
on Functioning, Session Themes)

                          NOTED!

PLANS / FOLLOW UP / QUESTIONS FOR SUPERVISION

NOTED!

Client: Time: to:

Session Date: Code:

                                 Next Session:

Session Focus

1

2

Client Data *(Symptoms, MSE, Impact*   Interventions / Concerns
on Functioning, Session Themes)

NOTED!

PLANS / FOLLOW UP / QUESTIONS FOR SUPERVISION

NOTED!

Client: **Time:**   to:

Session Date: **Code:**

                                         Next Session:

Session Focus

1

2

Client Data *(Symptoms, MSE, Impact*   Interventions / Concerns
on Functioning, Session Themes)

NOTED!

PLANS / FOLLOW UP / QUESTIONS FOR SUPERVISION

NOTED!

Client: **Time:**   **to:**

Session Date: **Code:**

                                               Next Session:

Session Focus

1

2

Client Data *(Symptoms, MSE, Impact*   Interventions / Concerns
on Functioning, Session Themes)

NOTED!

PLANS / FOLLOW UP / QUESTIONS FOR SUPERVISION

NOTED!

Client: **Time:**   **to:**

Session Date: **Code:**

                                               Next Session:

Session Focus

1

2

Client Data *(Symptoms, MSE, Impact*   Interventions / Concerns
on Functioning, Session Themes)

NOTED!

PLANS / FOLLOW UP / QUESTIONS FOR SUPERVISION

NOTED!

Client: Time: to:

Session Date: Code:

                                                  Next Session:

Session Focus

    1

    2

Client Data (*Symptoms, MSE, Impact*   Interventions / Concerns
on Functioning, Session Themes)

NOTED!

PLANS / FOLLOW UP / QUESTIONS FOR SUPERVISION

NOTED!

Client: **Time:**   **to:**

Session Date: **Code:**

                                                        Next Session:

Session Focus

1

2

Client Data *(Symptoms, MSE, Impact*   Interventions / Concerns
on Functioning, Session Themes)

NOTED!

PLANS / FOLLOW UP / QUESTIONS FOR SUPERVISION

NOTED!

Client: **Time:**   **to:**

Session Date: **Code:**

                                           Next Session:

Session Focus

1

2

Client Data *(Symptoms, MSE, Impact*   Interventions / Concerns
on Functioning, Session Themes)

NOTED!

PLANS / FOLLOW UP / QUESTIONS FOR SUPERVISION

NOTED!

Thank You!

about the author

Amanda Fludd is a Licensed Clinical Social Worker of 15+ years with a group Private Practice in NY. She has mastered her teaching skills with hundreds of hours supervising and training clinicians and students as a Clinical Supervisor, Adjunct Professor at Fordham Univesity Graduate School of Social Service (her alma mata) and while working at a state psychiatric hospital for over ten years, creating clinical documentation standards (and passing state audits).

Mrs. Fludd is passionate about collaborative learning processes, creating continuing education opportunities, and infusing her clinical experience and expertise to make learning easy and accessible. She conducts engaging training workshops focusing on documentation and record-keeping, clinical skills, self-development, and mindset tools to empower women in business. She is also a corporate mental health and wellness trainer for schools and organizations.

A proud Nassau/Suffolk ABSW member, mom of two (Malcolm & Safiya), wife to Keith, and one of the few that can call herself a Marathoner.

Contact us

 support@amandafludd.com

facebook.com/therapyisdope

instagram.com/therapyisdope
@amanda.fludd

www.linkedin.com/in/amanda-fludd/

To learn more about Amanda and her current projects. go to www.amandafludd.com

Noted!

PRINTED IN THE UNITED STATES OF AMERICA

FIRST PRINTING, 2023

ISBN: 9798397997751
IMPRINT: INDEPENDENTLY PUBLISHED

WWW.AMANDAFLUDD.COM

NOTED!

Made in the USA
Las Vegas, NV
25 September 2023

78107408R00045